Table of Contents

INTRODUCTION	2
CHAPTER 1: INTRODUCTION TO LOGISTICS	4
CHAPTER 2: SUPPLY CHAIN MANAGEMENT	6
CHAPTER 3: TRANSPORTATION IN LOGISTICS	8
CHAPTER 4: WAREHOUSING AND INVENTORY MANAGEMENT	10
CHAPTER 5: LOGISTICS PLANNING AND STRATEGY	12
CHAPTER 6: LOGISTICS TECHNOLOGY AND AUTOMATION	14
CHAPTER 7: GLOBAL LOGISTICS	16
CHAPTER 8: SUSTAINABLE LOGISTICS	18
CHAPTER 9: RISK MANAGEMENT IN LOGISTICS	20
CHAPTER 10: FUTURE TRENDS IN LOGISTICS	22
CHAPTER 11: CASE STUDIES AND REAL-WORLD EXAMPLES	24
CONCLUSION	27

Chapter 1: Introduction to Logistics

1. What is logistics?

Logistics is about planning and managing how goods, services, and information move from one place to another, starting from where they are made to where they are needed.

2. Why is logistics important?

Here are some reasons why logistics is important:

Saves Money: Good logistics helps reduce costs.
Happy Customers: Delivering things on time makes customers happy.
Beating the Competition: Companies with better logistics can offer better service.
Helps the Economy: Efficient logistics reduce waste and improve supply chains.

3. How has logistics changed over time?

Here is how logistics has changed over time:

Old Days: Logistics was used in wars to move troops and supplies.
Industrial Revolution: Trains and steam engines sped up transport.
Global Markets: With bigger markets, logistics became more complex.
Today: Technology like the internet helps track goods and automate tasks.

4. What are the main parts of logistics?

The main parts of logistics include:

Logistic Basics Q&A

by

Pinnacle Press

Introduction

Logistics is a key part of every business, ensuring products and information move smoothly from start to finish. Despite its importance, it is often misunderstood or overlooked. This book, "Logistics Basics Questions & Answers," aims to make logistics easy to understand for students, professionals, and business owners alike.

The book explains what logistics is, how it connects with supply chains, and the role of transportation, warehouses, and inventory management. It also looks at how technology is changing logistics, the challenges of global shipping, and the growing need for eco-friendly practices. Readers will learn how to manage risks and stay updated on new trends shaping the future of logistics.

Written in a simple question-and-answer style, the book includes real-world examples and practical advice. Understanding logistics is important for making better decisions and staying ahead in business, and this book provides the tools to do just that. Welcome to "Logistics Basics: Questions & Answers," a guide to understanding the foundation of modern business.

Transportation: Moving goods by road, rail, air, or sea.
Warehousing: Storing goods until they are sent out.
Inventory Management: Keeping track of stock to avoid running out or having too much.
Order Fulfillment: Receiving, packing, and delivering orders.
Logistics Information Systems: Using technology to track and plan logistics.
Reverse Logistics: Managing product returns and recycling.

Chapter 2: Supply Chain Management

1.a. How are logistics and supply chain management connected?

Logistics is a part of supply chain management. Logistics handles moving and storing goods, while supply chain management looks at the whole process, from getting raw materials to delivering finished products to customers.

1.b. What is their relationship?

Integration: Logistics works inside supply chain management to keep everything moving smoothly.
Teamwork: Logistics needs to work with suppliers, manufacturers, and retailers.
Same Goals: Both aim to save money, work efficiently, and keep customers happy.

2. What does supply chain management do?

Planning: Predicting demand and organizing resources.
Sourcing: Choosing and working with suppliers.
Production: Managing manufacturing processes.
Delivery: Making sure products reach customers on time.
Returns: Handling returns and product recalls.

3. How does supply chain management help logistics?

Here are ways supply chain management help logistics:

Better Information: Real-time updates on inventory and shipments.

Lower Costs: Smarter sourcing and production mean cheaper transport and storage.
Quick Changes: Easier to adapt to market changes.
Good Partnerships: Strong teamwork helps logistics run smoothly.

4. What problems can supply chain management face?

Supply chain management can face the following problems:

Complicated Systems: Dealing with many people, rules, and steps.
Demand Changes: When customer needs change suddenly, it's hard to keep up.
Disruptions: Events like bad weather or political issues can cause delays.
New Technology: Learning and using new tools takes time and money.

Chapter 3: Transportation in Logistics

1. What are the main ways to transport goods and what are their advantages and disadvantages?

Road: Trucks and vans move goods on highways and local roads.

Advantages: Flexible and reaches remote places.
Disadvantages: Traffic delays and higher costs.

Rail: Freight trains carry large loads over long distances.

Advantages: Cheaper for big shipments and eco-friendly.
Disadvantages: Limited routes and slower delivery.

Air: Planes transport goods quickly.

Advantages: Fast and great for perishable or valuable items.
Disadvantages: Expensive and limits on weight.

Sea: Cargo ships move goods across oceans.

Advantages: Best for big, heavy shipments.
Disadvantages: Slow and depends on ports.

Pipelines: Used for liquids and gases.

Advantages: Cheap to run and works nonstop.
Disadvantages: Only for certain products and costly to set up.

2. How do companies decide which method to use?

Cost: How much does it cost to ship?
Speed: Does it need to get there quickly?
Distance: How far does it need to go?
Type of Goods: Is it heavy, fragile, or needs special care?
Delivery Time: When does the customer need it?

3. How does technology help with transportation?

Technology can help with transportation in the following ways:

Tracking: GPS helps see where goods are in real time.
Better Routes: Software finds faster and cheaper ways to deliver.
Automation: Machines speed up loading and unloading.
Data Analysis: Helps spot problems and improve processes.

4. What problems does transportation face?

Here are some problems that transportation face:

Traffic: Busy roads can delay deliveries.
Rules: Different regions have different rules to follow.
Fuel Prices: Rising fuel costs increase shipping expenses.
Environment: Companies work to lower pollution from transport.

Chapter 4: Warehousing and Inventory Management

1. What is warehousing?

Warehousing means storing goods in a facility until they are ready to be sent to customers or retailers.

2. What are the main jobs of warehousing?

The main jobs of warehousing are:

Storage: Keeping goods safe until needed.
Inventory Management: Keeping the right amount of stock.
Order Fulfillment: Packing and shipping orders quickly.
Cross-Docking: Moving goods from one truck to another without storing them for long.
Extra Services: Some warehouses handle labeling, packaging, and checking product quality.

3. How is inventory management connected to logistics?

Here is how inventory management is connected to logistics:

Balancing Stock: Keeps enough stock to meet demand but avoids having too much.
Lower Costs: Reduces storage and insurance costs.
Transport Planning: Helps plan when and how to move goods.
Happy Customers: Makes sure products are ready for orders.

4. What are the best ways to manage inventory?

Here are the best ways to manage inventory:

ABC Analysis: Group stock by importance (A = high value, C = low value).
Just-In-Time (JIT): Keep only what you need when you need it to save storage space.
Regular Checks: Do audits to catch mistakes or losses.
Use Technology: Inventory software can track stock and improve accuracy.
Forecast Demand: Use data to predict how much stock is needed.

5. What problems happen with warehousing and inventory management?

Here are the problems that happen with warehousing and inventory management:

Space Issues: Making the most of warehouse space can be tricky.
Stock Errors: Mistakes in records can lead to problems.
Worker Challenges: Finding and keeping skilled workers is hard.
Using New Tech: Adopting new tools can take time and money.

Chapter 5: Logistics Planning and Strategy

1. What is logistics planning?

Logistics planning is the process of figuring out the best way to move and store goods efficiently. It involves organizing resources like vehicles and warehouses and preparing for possible problems.

2. Why is logistics planning important?

Here are the reasons why logistics planning is important:

Efficiency: Reduces delays and costs by optimizing schedules and routes.
Better Use of Resources: Ensures vehicles, warehouses, and other tools are used effectively.
Preparing for Problems: Helps avoid issues by planning for disruptions.
Happy Customers: Ensures on-time deliveries and accurate orders.

3. How can businesses create a logistics strategy?

Here are way businesses create a logistics strategy:

Look at Current Processes: Check how things work now and find areas to improve.
Set Clear Goals: Decide what you want to achieve, like faster deliveries or lower costs.
Track Performance: Use measures like delivery times and stock levels to monitor success.
Use Technology: Tools like route planning and warehouse software can improve operations.
Work Together: Talk with suppliers and customers to align goals.

Review and Improve: Test the strategy, track progress, and adjust when needed.

4. What tools help with logistics planning?

Here are tools that help with logistics planning:

Demand Forecasting: Predict future needs using past data.
Route Planning Software: Find faster, cheaper delivery routes.
Inventory Tools: Keep track of stock and automate orders.
Simulation Models: Test different plans to see what works best.
Lean Methods: Remove waste to make processes simpler and faster.

5. What challenges can arise in logistics planning?

Here are some challenges that can arise in logistics planning.

Bad Data: Wrong or old data can lead to poor decisions.
Market Changes: Sudden changes in demand or supply can disrupt plans.
Limited Resources: Small budgets or not enough staff can slow improvements.
Tech Problems: New tools can take time, money, and training to set up.

Chapter 6: Logistics Technology and Automation

1. What types of technology are used in logistics?

Here are common technologies used in logistics:

Transportation Management Systems (TMS): Software for planning and tracking shipments, choosing carriers, and checking costs.
Warehouse Management Systems (WMS): Tools to manage inventory, orders, and workers in warehouses.
ERP Systems: Software that connects logistics with other business functions like finance and HR for better visibility.
Real-Time Tracking: GPS and sensors that let companies track shipments as they move.
Robotics and Automation: Robots and automated machines that speed up work in warehouses.
Data Analytics: Tools to analyze trends, predict demand, and improve decisions.

2. How is automation changing logistics?

Here are some ways automation is changing logistics:

More Productivity: Machines handle repetitive tasks faster.
Lower Costs: Automation reduces errors and labor expenses.
Better Accuracy: Improves tracking stock and order accuracy.
Flexible Scaling: Easily adjusts to busy or slow times.
Safer Workplaces: Reduces risks of injuries by using robots for heavy tasks.

3. What are the benefits of logistics technology?

Here are the benefits of logistics technology:

Saves Time: Makes processes faster and smoother.
Better Decisions: Real-time data helps plan smarter.
Happy Customers: Accurate orders and tracking improve service.
Cost Savings: Reduces errors and labor costs in the long run.

4. What are the challenges of logistics technology?

The challenges of logistics technology include:

High Costs: Buying and setting up systems can be expensive.
Difficult Integration: Adding new tech to old systems can be tricky.
Employee Pushback: Workers may resist changes.
Data Security Risks: Protecting sensitive info is a big concern.

5. What are future trends in logistics technology?

Here are future trends in logistic technology:

AI and Machine Learning: For predicting demand and improving processes.
Blockchain: Tracks goods securely and transparently.
Greener Tech: Focus on electric vehicles and eco-friendly practices.
Drones and Driverless Vehicles: For faster deliveries.
Omnichannel Logistics: Offering smooth shopping across multiple platforms.

Chapter 7: Global Logistics

1. What are the unique challenges of global logistics?

The unique challenges of global logistics are:

Complicated Rules: Each country has different import/export laws, taxes, and paperwork, making it hard to manage.
Cultural Differences: Language barriers and different business practices can make communication tricky.
Infrastructure Issues: Some countries have poor roads, ports, or systems, causing delays.
Disruptions: Events like natural disasters or political issues can mess up supply chains.
Risks: Shipping goods internationally increases risks of theft, loss, or damage.

2. How do customs and regulations affect global logistics?

Customs and regulations affect global logistics in the following ways:

Following the Rules: Companies must follow each country's trade laws or face fines and delays.
Paperwork: Missing or wrong documents can stop goods at customs.
Taxes and Tariffs: Extra costs like duties and tariffs can impact pricing.
Trade Deals: Agreements between countries can make trade cheaper and faster.

3. What trends are shaping global logistics today?

Here are trends that are shaping global logistics today:

Online Shopping Boom: E-commerce is pushing for faster global deliveries.

Eco-Friendly Practices: Companies are choosing greener ways to transport goods.
Using Tech: AI and data tools are helping businesses make better decisions.
Closer Suppliers: Many businesses are moving production closer to home to avoid long-distance delays.
Risk Planning: More companies are preparing for unexpected problems.

4. How can companies manage global logistics better?

Here are ways companies can manage global logistics better:

Work with Experts: Partner with experienced logistics providers to handle international shipping.
Use Technology: Tools like tracking systems and logistics software make operations smoother.
Watch Shipments: Real-time tracking helps find and fix problems quickly.
Plan for Risks: Think ahead about possible problems and have backup plans.

Chapter 8: Sustainable Logistics

1. What is sustainable logistics?

Sustainable logistics is managing the movement and storage of goods in ways that protect the environment while benefiting businesses and society.

2. Why is sustainable logistics important?

Here are reasons why sustainable logistics is important:

Protects the Environment: Reduces pollution and saves resources.
Follows Rules: Helps meet strict environmental laws.
Saves Money: Efficient routes and less waste cut costs.
Improves Reputation: Attracts eco-conscious customers.
Ensures Long-Term Success: Supports future resource and business needs.

3. How can companies make logistics more sustainable?

Here are ways companies can make logistics more sustainable:

Smarter Routes: Use software to plan the shortest and most fuel-efficient paths.
Eco-Friendly Transport: Use electric vehicles, trains, or bikes to cut fossil fuel use.
Efficient Warehouses: Save energy with better layouts, LED lights, and smart systems.
Green Packaging: Use less packaging or materials that are biodegradable or recyclable.
Reverse Logistics: Create systems for returns, recycling, and reusing products.

Work with Partners: Team up with suppliers who also care about sustainability.

4. What are the benefits of sustainable logistics?

Here are the benefits of sustainable logistics:

Cleaner Environment: Cuts greenhouse gases and waste.
Lower Costs: Saves money with better routes and less waste.
Better Reputation: Builds trust with customers who value green practices.
Stronger Supply Chains: Makes businesses less dependent on limited resources.
Meets Regulations: Keeps the company within legal environmental limits.

5. What challenges do companies face with sustainable logistics?

Here are the challenges companies face with sustainable logistics:

High Starting Costs: Switching to green tech and practices can be expensive.
Complicated Systems: Managing sustainability across a global supply chain is hard.
Lack of Knowledge: Some companies don't know how or why to go green.
Tracking Progress: Measuring and reporting on sustainability can be tricky.

Chapter 9: Risk Management in Logistics

1. What risks are involved in logistics operations?

Here are the risks involved with logistics operations:

Transportation Risks: Goods can be lost, stolen, or damaged during shipping.
Supply Chain Disruptions: Events like natural disasters or strikes can delay or stop the flow of goods.
Compliance Issues: Breaking rules or regulations can lead to fines or shipment delays.
Market Risks: Changes in demand or material prices can mess up plans.
Cybersecurity Threats: Hackers or system failures can disrupt operations.

2. How can businesses manage logistics risks?

Businesses can manage logistics risks in the following ways:

Assess Risks: Regularly check for possible problems in transport, storage, or compliance.
Plan for Problems: Have backup plans for delays or disruptions.
Use Insurance: Cover losses from damaged or stolen goods.
Diversify Suppliers: Don't rely on one supplier to avoid big disruptions.
Use Technology: Track shipments in real time and analyze data for potential issues.
Train Staff: Teach employees how to spot and handle risks.

3. Why is insurance important in logistics?

Here are reasons why insurance is important in logistics:

Covers Losses: Protects against damage or theft during shipping.
Liability Coverage: Helps with claims from accidents or damaged goods.
Customs Protection: Reduces costs from delays or compliance problems.
Peace of Mind: Gives businesses confidence to operate without constant worry.

4. What are common mistakes in managing logistics risks and how do you avoid this?

Common mistakes in managing logistics risks and how you avoid this include:

Skipping Risk Checks: Not reviewing risks regularly can lead to surprises.
Avoid This: Do regular assessments to find new risks.
Ignoring Compliance: Overlooking rules can mean fines or delays.
Avoid This: Stay updated on all regulations.
Not Training Staff: Employees might not know how to handle risks.
Avoid This: Offer regular training on managing risks.
Forgetting About Partners: Suppliers or logistics partners can cause problems.
Avoid This: Check their reliability often.
Poor Communication: Miscommunication can slow responses to problems.
Avoid This: Keep communication clear and open between all teams.

Chapter 10: Future Trends in Logistics

1. What are the latest trends in logistics?

The latest trends in logistics are:

Going Digital: Technology like automation, AI, and IoT is making logistics faster and more efficient.
E-commerce Growth: Online shopping is pushing for faster deliveries and better ways to handle returns.
Sustainability: Companies are using eco-friendly methods to reduce their impact on the environment.
Using Data: Analytics are helping businesses make smarter decisions and improve forecasts.
Blockchain: Improves transparency and prevents fraud in supply chains.
Drones and Robots: Autonomous delivery solutions like drones are becoming more common for last-mile delivery.

2. How are consumers affecting logistics?

Consumers are affecting logistics by:

Wanting Speed: Customers expect fast deliveries, so companies are improving shipping methods.
Personalized Service: People want options that fit their preferences.
Online Shopping: E-commerce needs stronger systems for shipping and returns.
Green Choices: Customers prefer companies that care about the environment.

3. What is the future of logistics?

The future of logistics include:

More Automation: Robots and machines will handle more tasks in warehouses and transportation.
Better Tracking: Real-time updates will improve transparency and customer service.
Smarter Systems: IoT devices will create connected logistics networks that adjust automatically to changes.
Resilient Supply Chains: Companies will focus on flexibility to handle disruptions better.
Cybersecurity Focus: Stronger defenses will protect against digital threats.

4. What skills will logistics professionals need?

Logistics professionals will need these skills:

Tech Knowledge: Understanding tools like tracking systems and data software.
Data Analysis: Knowing how to use data to make smart decisions.
Flexibility: Being ready to adapt to new tools and changes.
Sustainability Expertise: Knowing how to run greener logistics operations.
Project Management: Leading logistics projects effectively.

Chapter 11: Case Studies and Real-World Examples

1. **What can we learn from successful logistics companies?**

Here are some successful logistics companies and what you can learn from them:

Amazon:

What They Do Well: Fast delivery and excellent customer service.
How They Do It:
Fulfillment centers are placed near customers for quick delivery.
Technology is used to plan routes and manage inventory.
Offers options like same-day delivery and drone deliveries.
Lesson: Focus on technology and customer satisfaction for an edge in logistics.

Zara:

What They Do Well: Quickly responding to changing fashion trends.
How They Do It:
Controls its own production and logistics.
Produces small batches to avoid overstock.
Restocks stores twice a week.
Lesson: Be flexible and fast to meet changing demands.

DHL:

What They Do Well: Innovative and eco-friendly logistics.
How They Do It:
Uses robots for warehouse tasks.
Focuses on sustainability with electric vehicles and better routes.

Tracks shipments in real-time with smart technology.
Lesson: Invest in innovation and sustainability to improve operations.

2. How do different industries handle logistics challenges?

Here is how different industries handle logistics challenges:

Retail (E-commerce):

Challenge: Fast delivery for many orders.
Solution: Use AI to manage stock and speed up order processing.

Manufacturing:

Challenge: Disruptions in supply chains.
Solution: Work with multiple suppliers and predict risks using data.

Food and Beverage:

Challenge: Keeping perishable items fresh.
Solution: Use temperature-controlled shipping and tracking tools.

Pharmaceuticals:
Challenge: Following strict transport rules.
Solution: Work with experts who ensure compliance and monitor conditions.

3. What mistakes do companies make in logistics, and how can they avoid them?

Not Using Data:

Problem: Decisions aren't based on facts, leading to inefficiencies.
Fix: Use data tools to improve planning and customer service.

Weak Supplier Relationships:

Problem: Unreliable suppliers disrupt the supply chain.
Fix: Build strong, communicative partnerships with suppliers.

Underestimating Costs:

Problem: Ignoring transport costs hurts profits.
Fix: Review all expenses and optimize routes and transport modes.

Resisting Change:

Problem: Sticking to old methods slows growth.
Fix: Embrace new tech and processes, and train employees for smooth transitions.

Conclusion

Logistics Basics Q&A has taken you through the basics of logistics, highlighting its importance in supply chain management and its impact on business success. We've covered everything from core principles to advanced technologies, global challenges, and sustainable practices, showing how logistics supports efficient operations and happy customers.

Throughout this journey, we've seen that good logistics management relies on smooth coordination within the supply chain, the adoption of new technologies, and a focus on sustainability. Managing risks effectively is also key to keeping operations steady when challenges arise.

Logistics is always changing, with new ideas and tools shaping the way we work. By staying curious, learning continuously, and connecting with others in the field, you can adapt to these changes and find opportunities for growth.

Thank you for joining this journey into the world of logistics. Whether you are starting out or building on existing knowledge, the lessons from this book can help you improve business operations and create better experiences for customers.

www.ingramcontent.com/pod-product-compliance
Lightning Source LLC
Chambersburg PA
CBHW070945220526
45469CB00007B/2529